S0-BLW-260

To
Our very special friends
Ildiko and Roger
With love, friendship
and
Best Wishes
for
A Happy New Year
Magda
December 31, 2007

True love is everlasting

*If You Truly Love Me*

# If You Truly Love Me

## Magda Herzberger

### Illustrations by
### Monica A. Wolfson

1st WORLD LIBRARY
The World's Publisher

Austin, Texas

# If You Truly Love Me

By Magda Herzberger
Poetry, Prose, and Music © 2007 Magda Herzberger
Illustrations © 2007 Monica A. Wolfson

1sr World Library, an imprint of
Groundbreaking Press
8305 Arboles Circle
Austin, TX 78737
512-657-8780
www.groundbreaking.com

Library of Congress Control Number: 2007929295
ISBN: 0-9793542-1-8

First Edition

Senior Editor
Barbara Foley

Book Design & Production
Amy Nottingham
Tim Spivey (music)

Cover Design & Production
M. Kevin Ford

Original Cover Illustrations
Monica A. Wolfson

Interior Illustrations
Monica A. Wolfson

All rights reserved. No part of this book may be reproduced or utilized in any form or by any means, electronic or mechanical, including photocopying or recording, or by any information storage and retrieval system, with-out permission in writing from the author.

*My book of love poems is dedicated
to my beloved husband Eugene
in celebration of our
60th Wedding Anniversary.*

# To My Beloved Husband

Sixty years ago
We took our marriage vow.
We were then a young loving couple ...
Truthful, honest,
And dedicated to each other.
Our wedding ceremony
Was simple and modest.
Through the passage of the years,
Our love grew stronger than ever ...
We walked together
On the path of life
Sharing our joys and tears.
We are bound forever
To each other.

My dear husband,
How can I ever thank you
For all the years of happiness,
For all your care, concern, and love?
I am so grateful
To the Almighty God above
For sending you my way!
With you I want to stay
Till the end of my last day ...
Even after all these many years
   of married life
I feel like a young bride,
Happy to be still at your side,
On our 60th Wedding Anniversary.

# Acknowledgements

I owe a deep debt of gratitude to my beloved husband, Eugene Herzberger, M.D.

My special thanks to my dear friend, Maggie Smith, C.D.T.

My gratitude and appreciation to my daughter, Monica A. Wolfson, M.E.D.T. for all her efforts in creating and drawing the cover and interior illustrations featured in my book.

I am most grateful for the constant support of my publisher, Brad Fregger, and my senior editor, Barbara Foley.

My deepest appreciation to Amy Nottingham for the design and layout, and to Tim Spivey for the music design for my book.

# Contents

# Preface

The most meaningful and valuable gift I could think of presenting to my beloved husband Eugene for our 60th Wedding Anniversary is this collection of love poems, which I wrote for him throughout the many years of our married life.

They are the expressions and manifestations of my deep love, passion, and friendship for my husband.

I have also included the musical scores I composed to some of the lyrics.

I am very thankful to the Almighty for sending the man of my dreams to me some 60 years ago. And I am looking forward to many more years of happiness, love, and companionship with my partner in life.

Magda Herzberger
November 21, 2006

# The Power of True Love

Seasons come and seasons go, bringing along changes. Beginnings and endings alternate with the passage of time. We long for constancy, but we know that uncertainty follows us everywhere because it is a part of human destiny. When we commit our hearts to genuine love, then we possess the golden key of eternity which can't be tarnished or altered by the passing years. In true love we find lasting comfort, peace, joy, and security.

To be fidel till death will us part,
To be bound forever to our beloved's heart,
Means to be registered for eternal favors
On heaven's distinguished, special chart.

# If You Truly Love Me

If you truly love me,
Do not count the lines on my face
Etched by the hand of time,
Ignore the gray strands in my hair
When I pass my prime.

If you truly love me,
Accept the imperfections of my body,
Detect in my eyes
The flawless, unaltered beauty
Of my affection and loyalty.

If you truly love me,
Find lasting youth
In my passionate heart,
Committed to you
Till death will us part.

If you truly love me,
Hold me in esteem and grace,
Tell me that I am
The most precious to you

On this earth's face.
If you truly love me,
Stand by my side
Through the advancing years,
And share with me
Your joy and tears.

If you truly love me,
Be a friend of my soul,
Let us pursue together
A worthwhile, common goal:
To love and to cherish each other,
Till for us the bell will toll.

# Celebration in November

The month of November is not the most popular time of the year for many people. It is a reminder that the beautiful season of fall is coming to its end. The trees are getting robbed daily of their leaves and the grass loses its luscious green color, turning reddish-brown. The colorful butterflies disappear, the frost shrivels the dainty petals of the flowers, and the gusty, cold winds freeze the shivering, soft earth.

Yet, for my husband and me, November is a very special, cherished month connected with a joyful event. Its twenty-first day marks our wedding anniversary.

Many years have passed by since we joined hands in Holy Matrimony. With the passage of each year we leave our youth more and more behind, but we don't care as long as our hearts are filled with love and affection for each other.

At each anniversary I like to ask my husband the same questions.

# Will You Still Love Me?

Will you still love me
When I grow old and gray?
Will you still recall
The young girl
You carried away
As your bride
On a rainy day
In Fall?
Will you still hold me tight
Like on our wedding night?
Or, will you forget
The first day we met
In Summer
When roses were blooming
And birds were singing?
Will our cheerful laughter
Still be ringing in your ears?
Will you still remember
All the happy years
We spent together?
Please keep the glowing light
In your heart, for me, forever.

# Permanency

True love's golden leaves
Are always in their prime.
With the passage of the years
Their beauty becomes sublime,
God protects them from the thieves of time.
They never detach
From the tree of affection,
Clinging forever to the branches of passion,
Bound to the trunk of honesty and truth,
Nourished by the sap of eternal youth.

# New Beginnings

There is always a twilight and a new dawn. Day is followed by night and night is followed by day. A resurrection takes place within us each day. We remember the past—it belongs to us, and yet we have to learn from the past so that we can grow in the present and also in the future. After the dark night there is daybreak.

# Daybreak

Come, my love,
The night is gone.
Yesterday slipped away
On the Milky Way
And the purple dawn put on
Its sapphire crown,
Ushering the new day
And making way
For the rising sun.
Let us resume
Our daily course
On life's terrain,
Let the returning light
Illuminate our sight
And start a new episode.
Let us decipher a part
Of the hidden code
Of creation,
On our temporary
Earthly station.

# Reflection

The flames of life
Surround your image ...
I see the Red Sea
In your tears ...
Sinking into its depths
I float in the drops of existence ...
When the fire subsides
The blue sky is reflected in your eyes ...
My heart cries no more ...
I leave the burning shore
Bathing in the warm rays of love ...
The white dove of peace
Is soaring in space ...
The universe is mirrored
In your face ...

# Heartbroken

In the darkness of my thoughts,
I try to find my way
Amidst the broken ruins
Of yesterday.
Among the shattered remnants
Scattered in my mind,
I look for joy and pleasures
Left behind,
But only dust and dripping tears I find.
Pain and sorrow
Cast their black shadow
Upon my soul.
Only a small candle of hope
Is still burning,

As a reminder
Of lost passion and yearning.
I fumble around,
Trembling with fear ...
My love, I wish you were here!
Let your beloved face appear
On the screen of my imagination.
Grant me a last happy dream,
And fill my failing heart
Once more with exultation.
Please come, my end is near,
And shed for me at least a tear.

# Attend My Heart

In the hidden garden of my soul
I planted my love...
Its roots took hold of my heart.
Come, my beloved,
And sprinkle with affection
The blooming flower of passion.
Don't let it fall apart...
Caress its delicate petals,
Inhale its intoxicating fragrance.
Don't let it die of thirst...
Please come and comfort me,
Or my heart will burst.

# Small Bouquet

I remember
The first bunch
Of delicate flowers
You brought me
At the end of Winter.

You carried the fresh fragrance
Of Spring
Into my room
With white snowdrops
In bloom.

# Fidelity

Winter's dreary hands
Touch my hair,
Weaving white filaments
Into my dark strands,
But I don't care.
My mind is still engulfed
In Summer's heat.
My strong heartbeat can tell
That flames of passion still dwell
In my heaving bosom.
My love for you is pure and fresh,
Like a new blossom.
Death will still my breath one day,
But my love for you will never die.
It will take root in the earth,
Giving birth to a fiery rose.

Come then, close
To my velvety head.
You will hear me
Whispering in your ear,
"I am yours, from here
To eternity.
Drop a tear
On my soft petals
To revive my heart.
No one can take me
From you ever apart."

# Imprint

Pale rose,
Your shriveled petals
Hang limply
On your mourning stem.
Even the bright diadem
Of the sun
Can't restore
Your beauty anymore.
Decay invaded your heart
And faded your vivid color.
Your friends are still sleeping,
But the willow is weeping,
And the early morning dew
Drops its tears upon you.

Symbol of love,
Once flaming red,
Now lifeless and dull,
You are on your deathbed.
But the memory
Of your exquisite fragrance
And loveliness
Is embedded in my soul,
To remind me
Of passion, youth,
Romance, divinity.

# Lost Forever

I heard your voice before
And now, I can't recognize it anymore.
It sounds so strange and cold
As though it grew rough and old.
Once you sang to me
The sweet melody of love.
But the cruel hands of the years
Tore it apart,
And left me since
With a piercing pain
And a broken heart.

# Illusion

In the dark room
No one stirred.
Only the sound
Of my fast breathing
I heard.
Fantasy was playing tricks on me ...
I thought you were here,
Listening to my pounding heart,
And feeling the warmth
Of my body.
But I was alone,
With the shadow
Of a distant memory.

# Song of Love - 1

Come through the golden field,
Let your heart yield
To my burning love.
Look at the blue sky above,
Follow the peeking sun ...
Come, my beloved,
Before the day is gone!
Press your warm lips against mine,
Let your eyes shine
With affection.
Ignite the fire of passion
And let it burn,
As long as our days will turn
On the wheel of life.

# Escape

Let us elope
And follow the ray of hope
To the altar of love.
The burning torch of our passion
Will be our guiding light,
Through the dark night
Of our flight.
Let us pray
On our way:

"Merciful God,
Whose invisible Hand
Steers our fate,
Lead us to the gate
Of happiness.
Pardon our selfishness,
Don't let us get lost,
And into eternal darkness tossed.
Help us to reach
Our ultimate goal,
To be one, in body and soul."

# *Lost Love*

My heart is stiff and cold,
Void of lust,
Waiting like a frozen lake
For Spring to break
Its hard crust.
Winter's snow hits my brow,
Chilling passion's glow.
My spirit cries
And desperately tries
To melt the blocks of ice,
By shedding warm tears
Upon the frosty hands of years.
Trapped in the claws of distress
And wrapped in the night of gloom,
I am on the edge of doom,

Longing for love's flames and tenderness,
Searching for the rays of happiness.
In the dark prison of my mind,
Ominous thoughts prowl
And black shadows crawl.
Melancholy engulfs my head,
The sparks of joy are dead.
Silence descends
Upon the desolate island of my soul,
As death slowly lands,
Showing its merciless, grinning face.
I am crushed, tossed, and dispersed in space.

# Infamy

You injured my heart,
Stamping on it cruelly,
Leaving behind bleeding wounds,
Pain, agony,
And the dark stain
Of impurity,
Dimming my life's beauty and glow.
The hollow grooves
Of your footprints show,
Like black marks impressed
On the virgin snow.

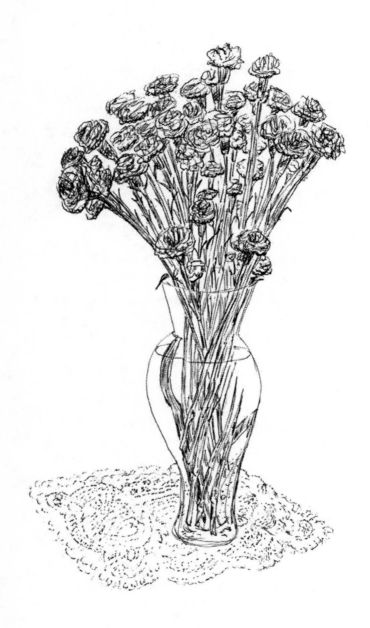

# Thoughts of Love

All of us are searching for True Love. When we find it, we then possess some of the magical and immortal properties of the eternal universe.

## United

You came to the threshold of my soul ...
I heard your call
And opened for you the door of love
To let you enter my heart ...
We grew on each other
From the start ...
And never after
Could we live apart.

# Let Me Rest
## Upon Your Chest

Let me rest
Upon your chest
My dearest...
Put your arm around my shoulder,
Clasp my hand.
Years passed by
But still, united we stand.
Let me rest upon your chest,
Hold me tight.
Your gentle touch
Opens the doors
Of joy and delight.

# Doomsday

My injured heart is ailing,
Its bleeding parts are wailing,
Anger's arrow pierced it through.
Come, my love, I wait for you
To ease my pain,
To cease the tortures of my brain.
Only you can undo the hurt,
Soothe my wounds, make me anew.
Heal with love my severed segments,
Unite all the torn fragments.
Give me a helping hand,
On the threshold of doom I stand.
But, if you ignore my call,
Refusing to hear my cry,
Then, I will die.

My soul will descend from the sky
To haunt you day and night.
My shadow will always be in sight
Staring at you with a mocking grin,
Reminding you of your sin.
When death's solemn bell
Strikes your last hour,
You will not see
The shining gates of heaven,
But the gaping pits of hell.

# Imprisoned

On silent nights
When the distant stars
Open their sparkling eyes,
And the yellow moon
Reveals its melancholic face,
The lonely heart cries
Locked in its cage,
Crippled by age,
A helpless prisoner of time...
But, once it was free and in its prime,
Beating with vigor
The fast rhythm of life...
And now, it is doomed and forsaken,
Its livelihood taken,
Robbed of love and pride,
Pushed aside,
Condemned to solitude...
Weary heart, where is your fortitude?
The hand of fate
Slammed on you
Its iron gate,
Extinguished your fire,

And left you to expire
In the prison of the years.
I hear your cry
And streaks of salty tears
Run down my cheeks ...
I turn to the lighted sky,
Asking for mercy ...
There is no reply.
But I can see from afar
The flashing light
Of a falling star ...
I mourn you,
Battered heart,
Slave of destiny,
Bound forever
In captivity.

# Reveries

Nostalgia and daydreaming are common human experiences. We like to relive past joyful episodes and indulge in wishful thinking. Our thoughts can travel through time and space, revitalizing us by reaching into the deep recesses of our minds where past events and feelings are stored. The spirit has freedom and magical powers to evoke pleasant scenes and emotions from the different stages of our life, making them real and touchable, bringing us comfort, contentment, peace, and happiness.

# Romance

Close your eyes and dream
Of green meadows,
Of blooming flowers,
Trees and shadows ...
Let your heart follow
Love's winding path
And in the sun's glow
Take a deep breath ...
Inhale the fragrance
Of life's sweet rose,
Fall into passion's
Enchanting trance ...
Evoke the spirit of young romance!
Let your thoughts travel
Through time and space,
Dream and unravel
Youth's charming face ...
Behold its beauty,
Its innocence,
Respect its purity,
Sense its presence ...
Let your mind wander

Through the fields of joy,
Look for old memories
Under the piles of years ...
Revive them one by one
With your warm tears,
And the sweet songs of love
Will reach your ears ...
You will hear whispers
Of young romance
And feel the ecstasy
Of enchanting trance!
Give your heart freely to reverie ...
Embrace and hold tight
A beautiful dream,
Drift with abandonment
In life's fresh stream ...
Hold on forever to your delight
And keep reality far out of sight!
Pain, grief, and sorrow will run away,
And your worn spirit will find its way
To the high mountains of happiness ...
Where true affection will be at your side,

Where truth and honesty
Will be your guide ...
Where passion's burning flames
Will warm your heart,
Where in the arms of love
A new life you will start ...
And in the wilderness of happiness,
Your long-departed youth will return to you
And will gently caress your injured soul,
Healing your bleeding wounds
With potions of joy ...
Cherished old memories
Time can't destroy.

# Happy Anniversary

A dozen red roses
You sent to me
This morning ...
The small card
Attached to them
I am reading:
  "To my loyal and beloved wife
  For our 20th Anniversary."
Many years have passed
Since the first day we met,
And yet, its memory
Never left me.
It remained intact,
Untarnished by time.
I recollect clearly
Being so young and innocent,
You were my teacher
And I, your admiring student.

You won my heart
From the start,
And became my guiding star.
Since then, we've come so far ...
Thanks for all these happy years,
My beloved husband.
This card for you I send
As my reply:
    "I will be your faithful, devoted,
    Loving wife, until I die."

# To My Husband

You've always worked hard
And never complained,
Your good spirits and strength
You've always maintained.
My beloved husband,
Words of thanks aren't enough
To show my appreciation.
I offer you my love,
My eternal dedication.

# My Love For You Is . . .

My love for you
Is like a mountain stream,
A constant, uninterrupted flow.
My love for you
Is like the sun's eternal glow.
Or like the sea,
Never at rest,
Gentle and forceful waves
Crossing endlessly
Its open breast.
My love for you is like a tree
Rooted in the heart.
True love belongs to eternity
And never falls apart.

# Rapture

The flames of love
Scorched my wings...
I am tied with the strings
Of ecstasy,
And carried to a world
Where I can't see anyone
But you and me,
Entwined in a tight embrace,
Riding on the ageless face
Of Eternity.

# Possessed

Lost in your arms
I succumb to your charms,
And submit to your fiery kisses
And soft caresses,
Abandoning my identity.
I am you and you are me ...
United in soul and body.

# Fascination

Come and be mine ...
Taste the sweet wine
Of love ...
And sense
The enchanting trance
Of divine romance!
Forget the years
Of agonies and tears...
Ride by my side
Day and night,
On the top of time,
Lost in sublime delight!

# End of Innocence

True love is smeared
With dirt and grime
And stoned to death
With the rocks of time.
Deceit's cruel hands
Committed the crime.
True love lies still
On the burial ground.
The wailing sound
Of the mourning dove
And the sad notes
Of a singing bird are heard.
The weeping trees
Whisper their eulogies,
They shed their leaves,
Covering the dead
With their green shroud.

A wandering cloud is passing by,
Carrying the loud cry of the wind
And the solemn proclamation of the sky:
"Innocence is slain,
The heart is filled with grief and pain.
True love is gone,
Seeing no more the rising sun.
Decadence will reign!"

# Condemned

Since you left me
I am desolate and lonely,
Like a deserted field
Of white snow
Where icy winds blow ...

I am left behind
With a frozen heart
And a tortured mind ...
In the cold wilderness of my soul,
I hear death's call.

# Revenge

You killed my love, and lust
Trampled on my heart
And turned me into dust ...
But I pushed the earth apart
Soon after ...
Choking your laughter,
Claiming your soul...
Making you pay for your crime
After all.

# Song of Love - II

There is a Paradise on earth
Where love gives birth
To happiness and joy ...
Where angels fly above and cheer,
Where the sky is bright and clear,
Where white doves of peace appear,
Where sweet heavenly songs are born,
Where Cupid blows his magic horn
And throws his arrows
Of flaming passion
And deep affection
In every possible direction ...
Where gentleness and kindness dwell,
Where you succumb to a magical spell ...
Where you seek and find
Contentment and peace of mind ...
Where you can turn in your hour of doom
From the confinement of your room,
And leave behind your bitter tears
And all the heartaches of past years ...

Where clinging to your lover's heart,
A wondrous journey you will start,
On the wings of ecstasy
And in the arms of reverie ...
During your ecstatic ascent,
You will inhale passion's intoxicating scent ...
When you reach Amour's Holy Land,
With your beloved, hand in hand,
You will understand
That love is a Sacred Covenant
And a precious gift
Of the distant firmament ...
Then you will sing the Song of Love
With the angels from above.

# Infatuation

Love's exulting melody
Pulsates in my heart ...
Life beats its fast rhythm
In my heaving bosom ...
Reason pounds in vain
In the deep recesses of my brain ...
The raving flame of passion
Engulfs my thoughts ...
I succumb to desire
Melting in its hot fire ...

# Flight

Harness my soul
To your spirit,
And let it carry
Your heavy burden
Of sorrow ...
Ride with me
To the sunny hills
Of tomorrow ...
Hide your tears,
Abandon your fears,
And let us borrow
Life's joys and thrills ...
Drink with me
The sweet elixir of love,
And let the stars and moon above
Witness our happiness ...
Kiss me and hold me tight
In the stillness of the night ...

# Rebirth

My heart, filled with infinite love,
Burst in two ...
One part was me,
The other one you.
It could never become one anymore,
You tore it away from its core ...
But I wouldn't want it any other way
Since you came that blessed day.

# Ardor

Love, your arrow stirs my heart,
My grief and sorrow fall apart.
The flames of joy are rising high,
Burning my wish to die.
Driven by emotion
I leave the world of reason,
And led by Cupid's gentle hand,
I enter Pleasure's Wonderland.
In love's heavenly paradise
Sufferance dies.
My heart melts in the hot glow
Of your eyes.
Consumed by fervor,
I am yours forever.
Guide me to your golden throne,
Let me be reborn.
My beloved, king of my life's dawn,
Bestow upon me passion's jeweled crown,
And press upon my body
The magic seal of Eternity.

# Temptation

On a small island
In the midst of the vast sea,
Dwell the mean Sirens
Of melancholy ...
Beware of their sweet songs
Directed to you,
The demons of false love
Will pierce you through ...
Navigate safely,
Keep your mind cool,
Resist temptation,
Don't be a fool!
But if your heart yields
To luring passion,
Choking your reason,
You will be locked up
In the devil's prison ...
The evil spirits of deceit and treason
Will stab your heart,
Tearing you apart ...

The gnomes of darkness
Play their deadly games,
Hurling their victims
Into hell's hot flames ...
Please heed my warning,
Don't be seduced
And into ashes reduced ...
Follow the right course,
Don't stray away!
For your safety I pray.
Believe me!
My words are true ...
A trapped soul from below,
Blinded by purgatory's fiery-red glow,
Is speaking to you.

# Love's Marvel

The gift of true love never loses its great value, nor its magic. It is like a heavenly blessing, performing miracles.

If we love someone with the depth of our whole being, then the universe is reflecting itself in the eyes of the beloved.

This is what happens when I look into the eyes of my husband.

# Offering

Thousands of stars twinkle in your eyes,
Flooding with light, the black night ...
The bright moon is reflected
In your shining face, my beloved ...
The purple dawn bestows upon you
Its jeweled crown...
The rising sun is sending your way
Its first ray,
Bathing you in its warm bay ...
I can't give you
Such unearthly riches as these,
But please accept my humble gift
Of love and honesty.
I offer you my heart and loyalty.

# Song of Love - III

In the Magic Garden of Lust
High above the earth's solid crust,
Guardian angels hover above
The Sacred Paradise of Love.
They sustain the Flames of Passion
And protect the pearls of True Affection.
That is the place where we belong,
Far away from the earthly throng.
Come with me and you will see
The enchanting face of Eternity.

Let us yield our hearts to pleasure,
Let us shield Amour's Great Treasure,
Let us pray to be allowed to stay
And not to be chased away
From that blessed place,
Filled with such beauty and grace.
Let us ask that we be never forced to leave
Like those two sinners, Adam and Eve.

God will listen to our plea
And not inflict upon us any penalty,

If we make very sure
That our love is sincere and pure.
Almighty is patient, tolerant,
And kind to those
Who are spiritually close,
Whose love is not shattered
By the hard rocks of time,
Whose deeds are not stained
By dirt and grime,
Who are one in body and soul,
Who select honesty as their highest goal,
Who are not guided by jealousy,
Whose hearts are free
From greed and conceit
And exempt from deceit,
Who are not carried away by emotion,
Who practice discipline, loyalty, devotion,
Compassion and tolerance.

Those who comply
With these rules of acceptance
Will win the grand price of admittance
To Love's Sacred Paradise.
The Creator knows that genuine love
Of a special kind
Is hard to find.

Therefore, all the submissions
Are carefully analyzed
Before being finalized.
The admissions are reserved for only a few
Loving couples like me and you.

Our total commitment to each other
From now on, forever,
And our tight embrace
Will touch the heart
Of each ethereal, heavenly grace.
We will be happy and proud
To be in the company
Of the celestial crowd.
Only true affection
Can evoke God's help, approval,
And protection,
Lifting us upwards,
Into the right direction.

# Ecstasy

Come here
And whisper in my ear,
"I am yours."
Come near
And gently kiss my lips,
Tightly hold my arms.
Let us dream
And be carried
By the current of love's stream
To the Island of Ecstasy,
Where the fruits of delight
Are ready to be picked.
Let us reap the harvest
Of ardor's paradise
And consume the roots of exultation.
Let us succumb
To passion's heavenly sensation.

Come and let us leave behind
The Gray Kingdom of Reality
With its folly and wisdom.
Let us enter,
You and me,
Hand in hand,
The Magic Land of Eternity.
There love's ports, for us,
Will be widely open
And all our earthly bonds
Will suddenly be broken.

# Bewitched

Enchanting love,
Why do I listen to your call?
What is your goal?
Why do I follow your steps?
Where do you lead
My tortured soul?
Maybe to the dark, somber woods
Where hungry wolves howl and prowl,
Waiting for their prey ...
Yet, I want to stay with you
And go wherever you go,
Bound to your whimsical desire,
My heart burning in your hot fire
And blinded by your dazzling glow ...
Why am I so helpless
Under your spell?
I can't tell,
Nor, do I care to understand ...
Don't ever leave me,
Never let go of my hand.
Take me forever
To your magic land.

# To My True Love

Fifty-three years have passed by
Since our Wedding Day.
Through all this time
We crossed on our way
The rough and smooth roads
Of existence,
With courage, trust,
And persistence.
Although our youth is gone,
We still have together
Lots of enjoyment and fun.
I am yours forever!
I still feel like a young bride
At your side.
You are my love,
My partner in life,
And my best friend.
Happy Anniversary,
My beloved husband!

# To My Beloved Husband

Fifty-seven years have passed by
Since you and I joined hands
In Holy Matrimony ...
We are still lovers and best friends.
Our love is well preserved,
It was not blemished,
Neither stained or tarnished
By the hand of time...
It remained pure and fresh,
Free of grime.
We are solidly bound
To each other
With the firm, strong ties
Of affection and passion.
From now on, forever...

My dear husband,
To you I extend
My loving heart,
My devotion, my loyalty,
And my best wishes
For our fifty-seventh
Wedding Anniversary!

# A Lesson in Love

There is no place for true love
On this earth's face.
Strings are attached
To passion's wings ...
There is no room
For sweet and peaceful dreams
In a mind conquered by gloom.
But there is ample space
For nightmares and pain,
The deformed children
Of a tortured brain.
Don't tempt me
With false affection,
With fake loyalty,
With distorted honesty.
I know that you will not cry
If I die from deceit's foul play.
Betrayal chilled my heart ...
My hair turned gray,
My cheeks pale and hollow,
Death's winding path I follow ...
Soon, you will see me no more

On life's wild and rough shore.
After I am gone,
You will pursue your earthly fun.
But one day
Wisdom will knock on your door,
Finding its way to your heart ...
And you will discover
That you lost the one who loved you most.
Then, if you feel sad and lonely, call me ...
I will leave my resting place,
I will roam through time and space
Until I find your home.
I will kiss your face
And hold you tight,
Not letting you out of sight
Until you learn
That flames of passion within me still burn.
I will gently caress your hand,
Helping you to understand
That death's cold blow
Could not cool
My passion's glow.

Although my body was sealed
In earth's dark tomb,
Death's sharp claw could not pull out
Cupid's arrow
From my spirit's fertile womb,
Leaving it barren.
Because True Love is protected by God
And resides with the Angels in Heaven.

# To the Newlyweds

Happy bride and groom,
Before the altar of love you stand
In the House of God,
Hand in hand,
Waiting to be pronounced
Husband and wife.
Soon you will take
Your sacred vow of loyalty,
Entering together,
Side by side,
The roads of life
And the path of Eternity.
Your deep affection for each other
Will be your guide,
The flames of your ardent passion
Will burn your doubts and fears
Through the march of years.
The rays of happiness will glow
In your hearts,
Your tears of joy
Will destroy the trace of sorrow,
Clearing the face of tomorrow.

The song of love will echo
Wherever you go.
God bless you both
And sanctify your marriage oath!
May the Creator bestow upon you
Good luck, prosperity,
Eternal love, and fidelity.
May you always be dedicated to each other,
May your sacred union last forever.
May the Lord's benediction
Fall upon your heads today,
And be the guiding light
On your way.

# To My Dear Husband

Three angels from heaven
Came to me today,
Bringing these magic red roses
For your birthday.
There are no traces
Of blemishes
On these velvety, soft faces.
These magnificent perfect flowers
Bloom each day, high above.
They display their beauty
In the Paradise of Love.
They are imbibed and blessed
With a delightful heavenly scent,
Their delivery is a sacred event.
They contain in their delicate fragrance
The essence of love's magical potion,
Which evokes in us when inhaled,
Feelings of deep affection,
And great devotion.

I was told that they belong
To you and me,
Because our love is constant and strong,
Honest and pure.
Therefore, this card holds
The celestial signature ...
But it is written and signed by me,
Your loving wife,
Whose heart is committed to you
Till death will us part!

# Yours Forever

You ignite the flames of passion in my heart
When you start pressing hot kisses
Upon my burning lips and face,
Holding me in a tight embrace.
My mind and body are on fire,
I succumb to wild desire,
Clinging to your body
Like a leaf to a tree.
Don't ever leave me,
I am yours forever!
My love for you is stronger than ever,
It is forged in my heart
By the blazing torch of passion,
With utmost skill and perfection.
It is stamped in my soul
With the sacred seal of loyalty and affection.

My love for you is genuine, sincere,
Honest, and true,
It will never die!
It will always shine for you,
Like the sun, the stars,
And the moon in the sky.
Fifty-nine years have passed by
Since we joined hands in Holy Matrimony.
My beloved husband,
Happy Wedding Anniversary!
With you I want to stay
Till the end of my last day.
For many more happy years for us, I pray!

# Trapped

The memory
Of a distant
Winter night
Is haunting me
In the chambers
Of my heart.
I see the white
Frozen floating flakes above,
I hear the sweet
Melody of love.
I feel your arms
Around my shoulders,
The warm glow
Of your eyes
Melts winter's ice.
The memory
Of your love
Is still with me,
Holding my heart
In captivity.

# Trapped

Arranged by
Frank Metis

Words and Music by
MAGDA HERZBERGER

The mem-o-ry of a dis-tant win-ter night Is haunt-ing

Melody

Trapped

me in the cham-bers of my heart. I see the

white fro-zen float-ing flakes a - bove, I hear the

## Trapped

sweet    mel - o - dy of  love.      I  feel your

arms    a - round my  shoul - ders,    the warm glow

Trapped

of your eyes, – melts win-ter's ice.

The mem-o - ry          of your love is still with

Melody

Trapped

# Forsaken

Like a lonely star
Still blinking in dawn's
Purple sky,
So am I
Still burning
In the gray ashes
Of yesterday.
My heart still flares up
With passion and yearning,
Clinging to the last spark of fire,
Of a lost love and a dying desire.

# Forsaken

Arranged by
Frank Metis

Words and Music by
MAGDA HERZBERGER

Like a lone-ly star, Still blink-ing on dawn's pur-ple sky,

So am I, still burn-ing In the gray ash-es of yes-ter -

day. My heart still flares up with pas - sion and

# FORSAKEN

Like a lone-ly star, Still blink-ing on dawn's pur-ple sky,

So am I, So am I, So am I, So am

*a tempo*

*rall.*

# FORSAKEN

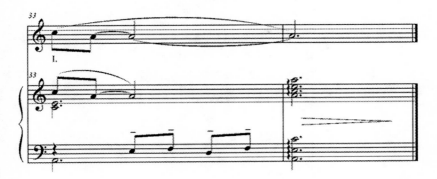

# Haunted

Where are love's flames?
Where is the fire
Of burning lust
And wild desire?
I must accept
The dry, cold dust
Of death's pyre ...
Riches of joy
And piles of pleasure,
Amor's white pearls
And passion's treasure
Are lost forever ...
But their shadows
Never leave me ...
They haunt my heart,
Pulling it apart,
With the rough strings
Of memory.

# Haunted

Arranged by
Frank Metis

Words and Music by
MAGDA HERZBERGER

Where are love's flames, Where is the fire of burn-ing

## Haunted

lust  And wild de - sire?  I  must ac - cept  the dry cold

dust  of death's  pyre.

# Haunted

Rich-es of    joy      And piles of pleas-ure,  A-mor's white   pearls  And pas-sion's  treas-ure  Are lost for -

# Haunted

# Haunted

heart,      Pull   it   a -   part      With   the   rough

strings    of   mem - o -   ry.      They   haunt   my    heart,     Pull   it   a -

part   With the rough   strings   of   mem  -  o  -  ry.

sadly

poco a poco ritard.     molto dim.     *p*        *pp*

# Out of Tune

Like a false melody
Painful to the sensitive ear,
So are the dissonant sounds
Of a dying passion
Coming near...
Distorted, disjointed,
Yet still alive,
Played over and over
By the untuned violins of the heart
With no end
But a start...
Until the strings break
And fall apart.

# Out of Tune

Arranged by
Frank Metis

Words and Music by
MAGDA HERZBERGER

# OUT OF TUNE

Pain - ful to the sen - si - tive ear, So are the

dis - so - nant sounds of a dy - ing pas - sion com - ing

## OUT OF TUNE

lins  of  the  heart.  With  no  end,  with  no  end,  with

no  end,  but  a  start...  Un - til the strings  break  and  fall  a -

part, Un – til the strings break and fall a – part.

poco a poco dim.

p

mp molto legato

ritard. e morendo

pp

8ves.

# Seduction

Don't leave me alone
On sorrow's throne
Wrapped in the shroud
Of pain and grief.
Don't let me dry
And shrivel up
Like a dead leaf.

Come and embrace me,
Warm up my cold heart.
Don't let my spirit
Fall apart.

Listen to me
And come quickly,
Before dark gloom
Strikes my sick soul,
Before the hand
Of cruel fate
Bores in my mind
A wide, deep hole.

Please come and take me
To Cupid's corner,
Beyond the border
Of doom.

Please hold me tight,
Caress my face
With tenderness,
Let me find peace,
Laughter and joy,
And happiness.

Let me abandon
The land of sorrow,
Let's roam the hills
Of bright tomorrow!

# Seduction

Arranged by
Frank Metis

Words and Music by
MAGDA HERZBERGER

Don't leave me a - lone on sor - row's

throne, Wrapped in the shroud of pain and grief. Don't let me

## Seduction

dry and shriv-el up like a dead leaf. Come and em-

brace me, Warm up my cold heart, Don't let my

# Seduction

Seduction

hand    of  cru - el    fate    bores  in  my    mind    a  wide, deep

hole.    Please come and    take  me    to  Cupid's cor - ner,

# Seduction

d me    Be-yond the  bor - der  of  doom.          Please hol

*poco rit.*

Let me find      tight, ca-ress my  face  with ten-der - ness,

*mf with motion*

## Seduction

peace, laugh - ter and joy and hap - pi - ness. Let me a-

ban - don the land of sor - row,

## Seduction

Let's roam the hills of bright to - mor - row.

*poco a poco ritard.*

# In Love

The rising sun
Kissed my eyes,
Melting my gloom,
And in my heart
Love started to bloom ...
I roamed the busy streets,
Passing the rushing crowd,
Calling your name aloud ...
I was aflame!
My burning lips were seeking yours
On those endless morning tours.
One day, I reached your place
And caught a glimpse of your face...
With open arms I ran to you
And finally my wish came true...
We walked hand in hand
In Love's Wonderland.

# In Love

Arranged by
Frank Metis

Words and Music by
MAGDA HERZBERGER

*Flowingly, with expression*

The ris-ing sun kissed my eyes, melt-ing my gloom. And in my heart love start-ed to bloom.

*legato*

*mp*

# In Love

## In Love

flame, My burn-ing lips were seek-ing yours On those end - less morn - ing

tours. One day I reached your place, And caught a

## In Love

glimpse  of  your  face.  With o - pen  arms  I ran to

you,  And fin - al - ly  my  wish came  true.  We walked  hand  in

## In Love

hand        in "Love's   Won - der - land."

# Eternally Yours

If we truly love someone, then we feel that even death can never separate us from our beloved. We will be resurrected by the power of Great Love.

We will emerge from the grave transformed into a different form of life, still seeking our beloved left behind, still yearning to experience, even for a short time, the tender touch, the deep affection, and the passion once shared.

# Resurrection

Bury me
Under the old willow tree ...
With dry earth
Cover me ...
Place then the tombstone ...
I will remain alone,
Dead flesh and bone ...
Come back sometime later ...
In my place
You will find a red flower ...
Pick me up,
Take me home ...
Place me in the fresh, cool water ...
Let me live again with you
For a few more days ...
Then, throw me away
When my petals and stem
Will decay ...

# Resurrection
## (Let Me Live Again With You)

For Solo Voice and S.A.T.B. Chorus

Arranged by
Frank Metis

Words and Music by
MAGDA HERZBERGER

# RESURRECTION (Let Me Live Again With You)

RESURRECTION (Let Me Live Again With You)

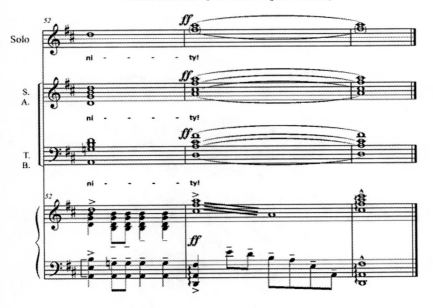

# About the Author

Magda Herzberger was born and raised in the city of Cluj, Romania. She is a poet, lecturer, composer, and the author of eight previously published books: *The Waltz of the Shadows* (1st and 2nd Editions), *Eyewitness to Holocaust, Will You Still Love Me?, Songs of Life*, and her most recent works, *Survival*, the compelling autobiography of Magda's early life in Romania and her suffering at the hands of the Nazis, *Devotional Poetry*, dedicated to the readers of *Survival*, and *Tales of the Magic Forest*.

Magda was a marathon runner, skier, and mountain climber. She and her husband, Dr. Eugene Herzberger, a retired neurosurgeon, reside in Fountain Hills, Arizona. They have a daughter Monica, a son Henry, and two grandchildren.

Magda's primary goals are to instill love for poetry in the hearts of people through her work, to keep the memory of the Holocaust alive, and to show the beauty of life through her writings and music. Her philosophy of life: Have faith, hope, and love in your heart—believe in impossible dreams and make them come true—cherish each moment of life—and never take anything for granted.

Groundbreaking Press, publisher of *If You Truly Love Me* and *Survival*, also publishes the Second Edition of *The Waltz of the Shadows*, *Devotional Poetry*, and, her first children's book, *Tales of the Magic Forest*.

Magda may be contacted at:
magdaherzberger@yahoo.com
www.magdaherzberger.com

# About the Illustrator

The cover and interior illustrations for *If You Truly Love Me* have been created by Monica A. Wolfson. Monica is Magda Herzberger's daughter. She also created the cover and inside illustrations for Magda's books *Devotional Poetry* and *Tales of the Magic Forest*.

Monica has a Masters from Arizona State University in Educational Technology. She is also an accomplished singer, having performed in various venues, and having written and published her own songs and poetry. In addition to all of the above, she is a professional photographer.

Monica is married to Dave Wolfson, a transportation planner and committed storm chaser and photographer. They live in Fountain Hills, Arizona.

Monica can be contacted at:
monica@wolfsonworks.com
www.wolfsonworks.com

Printed in the United States
89226LV00003B/7-54/A